THE MUMMY

BY IAN THORNE
ADAPTED FROM THE SCREENPLAY BY JOHN L. BALDERSTON

EDITED BY
DR. HOWARD SCHROEDER
Professor in Reading and Language Arts
Dept. of Elementary Education
Mankato State University

Library of Congress Catalog Card Number: 81-12481
International Standard Book Numbers:
0-89686-186-4 Library Bound
0-89686-189-9 Paperback
Design - Doris Woods

Library of Congress Cataloging in Publication Data

Thorne, Ian. Adapted from the screenplay by John L. Balderston
  The Mummy.

  (Monster series)
  SUMMARY: Recounts the plots of the 1932 Boris Karloff thriller "The Mummy" and of several later films in which ancient mummies return to life.
  1. Horror films--History and criticism--Juvenile literature. (1. Horror films. 2. Mummies--Fiction) I. Schroeder, Howard. II. Title. III. Series: Thorne, Ian. Monsters series.
  PN1995.9.H6T53   791.43'09'0916   81-12481
  ISBN 0-89686-186-4 (lib. bdg.)   AACR2
  ISBN 0-89686-189-9 (pbk.)

PHOTOGRAPHIC CREDITS

Universal: 9, 10-11, 12, 15, 16-17, 18, 19, 20, 21, 22-23, 25, 26, 27, 28, 29, 30, 31, 32, 33, 34, 47
Ackerman: Cover, 2, 6, 37, 38-39, 40, 41, 42, 43, 44, 45

Published by arrangement with MCA PUBLISHING,
A Division of MCA Inc.

MCA PUBLISHING, a Division of MCA Inc.
100 Universal City Plaza
Universal City, California 91608
Published by
CRESTWOOD HOUSE, INC.
Highway 66 South
P.O. Box 3427
Mankato, Minnesota 56002-3427
Printed in the United States of America

THE MUMMY

BY IAN THORNE
ADAPTED FROM THE SCREENPLAY BY JOHN L. BALDERSTON

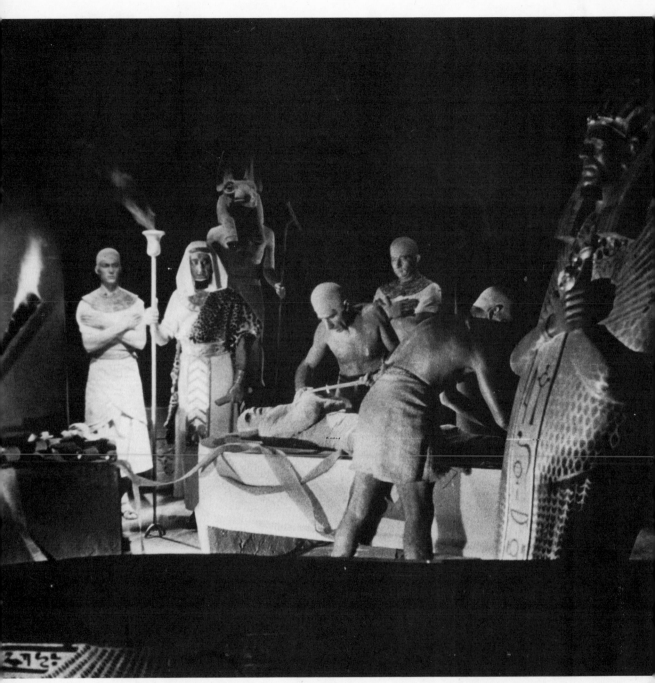

The inner coffin of King Tutankhamen's mummy was made of solid gold.

MUMMIES OF ANCIENT EGYPT

You can see them in many large museums.

Often, there is a large coffin made of stone. Inside, is a wooden coffin shaped like the body of a man or woman. This may be painted or even decorated with gold. And inside that . . . a mummy. A preserved body, thousands of years old, wrapped in crumbling bandages. The mummy could have been a king or a queen, a noble man or woman, a scientist, a great soldier, or a teacher. Ancient Egyptians believed that they would live on in the Land of the Dead — but only if their bodies had been preserved as mummies.

After death, the body was treated with chemicals. It was wrapped in fine linen with spices and perfumes. The coffin was the finest that the family could afford. With the coffin were food, clothing, and furniture — and sometimes gold.

The mummy of King Tutankhamen was found in 1922. With it was a fabulous golden treasure. Some of the people who found the tomb died not long afterward. Newspapers began to talk about "the mummy's curse." This idea inspired many stories, and also some of the best horror movies ever made.

The classic thriller is *The Mummy,* starring Boris Karloff. Made in 1932, it was written by John L. Balderston.

. . . Three men had made a great discovery!

It was the year 1921. An expedition from the British Museum was in the desert of Egypt, looking for ancient tombs. And now the diggers had found one!

Sir Joseph Whemple, the leader, entered the musty stone chamber. His assistant, Ralph Norton, and another scientist named Dr. Muller followed.

"Look! There is a mummy case!" exclaimed Sir Joseph. He studied the Egyptian writing. "It dates from the time of Pharaoh Amenophis, 3,700 years ago."

Eagerly, the three men opened the case. "His name was Im-ho-tep," Sir Joseph said. "But, what's this?"

He drew back in surprise. The tall figure in the case was swathed in crumbling bandages up to the neck. But the head was uncovered and turned to one side.

Dr. Muller gave a gasp. "This man was buried alive!"

Near the mummy case stood a small golden casket. Dr. Muller stooped to read the writing on it.

"Listen to this!" he said. "It's a curse: *DEATH. ETERNAL PUNISHMENT FOR ANYONE WHO OPENS THIS CASKET.*"

Dr. Muller (Edward Van Sloan) and Sir Joseph Whemple (Arthur Byron)
discuss plans before entering the tomb.

9

Ralph Norton (Bramwell Fletcher), Dr. Muller and Sir Joseph Whemple examine the Mummy.

Young Ralph Norton burst out laughing. "What nonsense!" He reached for the lid of the casket.

"No, Ralph," said Sir Joseph. "We won't open the casket yet. Perhaps later."

"What could be inside?" Norton wondered.

"Perhaps," said Dr. Muller, "it contains a clue to Im-ho-tep's terrible death."

Later, the mummy in its case and the strange

The Mummy (Boris Karloff) reaches for the scroll while Norton watches
in amazement.

golden casket were brought out of the tomb to be studied. Late one night, Ralph Norton was alone in the field laboratory. He could not resist opening the casket.

Inside was a scroll.

Eagerly, Norton spread the ancient piece of paper on a desk. He began to read it aloud.

"O Amon Ra. O god of gods. Death is but a doorway to new life. We live today. We shall live again. In many forms shall we return . . ."

The casket contained the legendary Scroll of Thoth, with the magic spell used by the Goddess Isis to raise her brother, Osiris, from the dead.

Norton continued to read aloud. He did not realize that the spell was working! Behind him, the ancient mummy of Im-ho-tep stirred. One eye opened. The hands in their moldy bandages began to move.

Absorbed in the scroll, Norton noticed nothing wrong. And then a hand — thin as a skeleton's, with wrinkled, dry flesh, wearing a strange ring — reached out to touch the scroll!

Norton turned and saw who was standing there. For an instant, his face twisted in terror. Then he leaped back and began to laugh insanely. He was still laughing as the mummy picked up the Scroll of Thoth and walked out the door.

After a time, Sir Joseph and Dr. Muller returned. They found poor Ralph Norton, turned into a raving madman. He could not stop laughing.

"He went for a little walk," Norton giggled. "You should have seen the look on his face!"

. . . Ten years went by.

Sir Joseph Whemple became the head of the Cairo Museum. His son, Frank, grew to manhood and took over the exploration work that Sir Joseph had once done. Frank had been searching in vain for the tomb of the Princess Ankh-es-en-amon. He was ready to give up. But then a strange, tall man walked into the camp. He was remote and dignified, with burning eyes and a deeply wrinkled face.

"I am Ardath Bey," said the mystery man. "I will show you where to dig."

The weird old man refused to shake hands with Frank. But he spoke with such assurance that the young scientist followed his directions. The digging crew went to work, and within a short time they had uncovered the entrance to the princess's tomb.

Frank was overjoyed. "Ardath Bey!" he called. "You were right! We've found her!"

But the strange visitor had disappeared.

Frank wasted no time worrying about him. He prepared to transfer the remains of the princess to the museum at Cairo.

Ardath Bey (Boris Karloff) shows young Frank Whemple (David Manners) and his assistant (Leonard Mudie) where to dig.

15

Ardath Bey broods over the mummy of the princess.

The mummy of Princess Ankh-es-en-amon was placed in a glass case for visitors to admire. Two people seemed especially interested. One was young Helen Grosvenor, daughter of the Governor of Sudan.

Another was a very tall man with a wrinkled face.

One night, the tall man hid when the museum closed. Later he came out and knelt beside the case where the princess's mummy lay.

In a trance, Helen Grosvenor (Zita Johann) leaves the party.

It was Ardath Bey. He had with him the Scroll of Thoth. He began to recite its life-giving spell:

"Death is but a doorway to new life . . . We shall live again. In many forms we shall return."

At the same time, many miles away, Helen was giving a party. Suddenly she felt strange. Someone seemed to be calling her. Unable to help herself, she rushed to the museum and tried to get in. But the doors were locked.

"Im-ho-tep!" she cried.

At that moment, inside, a museum guard had come upon Ardath Bey kneeling beside the princess's mummy. The guard thought Ardath had stolen the scroll and grabbed it. Furious, the tall man raised his hand. A mysterious force struck the guard. He cried out and fell to the floor, lifeless.

The dead guard is found.

Frank Whemple (David Manners) finds Helen on the museum steps.

Meanwhile, outside, Frank Whemple had come upon Helen. She had collapsed on the museum steps. Frank took her home, where she was treated by her doctor. He was none other than the Dr. Muller who had helped to find Im-ho-tep's tomb ten years earlier.

Sir Joseph and Dr. Muller met Frank at Helen's home. They had the scroll, which had been clutched in the dead guard's hand. Sir Joseph recalled that Ardath Bey used to visit the mummy of Ankh-es-en-amon.

Dr. Muller said, "Ardath knows something about this crime. He is not what he seems! I don't think that the mummy of Im-ho-tep was stolen with the scroll ten years ago. I think — "

Just then, the three men heard Helen, talking in another room. Someone had come to see her. And his voice was familiar.

The men rushed in. "Ardath Bey!"

The Egyptian was staring at Helen. She seemed to be in a trance.

Helen and Ardath Bey gaze at each other.

"What are you doing here?" cried Frank.

Ardath paid no attention. He said softly to Helen:
"We shall live again. In many forms we shall return . . .
And you have come back to me, my Princess! You live

Ardath Bey talks quietly to Helen as the others listen.

in the body of Helen Grosvenor."

"We know who you are, Ardath Bey," said Dr. Muller. "The Scroll of Thoth brought you back to life. YOU are Im-ho-tep!"

The wrinkled man with the burning eyes turned to Sir Joseph. "You have something that belongs to me." He held out his hand for the scroll.

"No!" cried the museum director. "What have you been doing to Helen?"

"She, too, belongs to me," said Ardath. "In another life, she was my beloved, Ankh-es-en-amon. She does not remember me now. But the power of the scroll will reunite us. Give it to me!"

Ardath raised one hand. On a finger gleamed a magic jewel. "Give me the scroll!" said Ardath. A ray from the jewel struck Sir Joseph. He fell unconscious.

Dr. Muller scooped up the scroll. He rushed to the fireplace and held the paper close to the flames. "Get out!" he shouted. "Get out, or I'll burn the scroll!"

Ardath lowered his hand. His scowl was awesome. "Very well. But sooner or later I will have what belongs to me!"

Ardath Bey asks Sir Joseph for the scroll.

Time passed. Ardath Bey seemed to have vanished. But he was still at work. The mummy of Ankh-es-en-amon was stolen from the museum! And Helen continued to act very strange. Sir Joseph decided to burn the scroll, even though it was very valuable.

In another part of the city, Ardath sat in his mansion. He stared into a pool of water — and in it was an image of Sir Joseph.

Ardath casts a death spell through the magic pool.

Across the city, Sir Joseph has a fatal heart attack.

Ardath saw Sir Joseph beside his fireplace with the scroll. The Egyptian's hand reached out toward the water. It twisted— squeezed — and the reflection of Sir Joseph grabbed at its chest.

Far away, the real Sir Joseph cried out. His heart seemed to burst. He slumped to the floor and died. Moments later, his Nubian servent came into the room. He took the scroll.

Ardath thanks the servant
for bringing the scroll.

Later, the servant brought the magic roll of paper to Ardath Bey. "You have done well," said the living mummy. "And now . . . Helen."

Once again, he looked into the enchanted pool.

Back home, Helen heard his mystic call and could not resist it. She came through the Cairo Streets to Ardath's mansion, where he waited for her in the room with the pool.

Suddenly, Helen came to her senses. "Who are you? What am I doing here?"

"I am Im-ho-tep! Come. Look into the water and you will remember your other life. The life you lived as Princess Ankh-es-en-amon."

Helen cannot resist Ardath's summons and comes to the pool.

Im-ho-tep (Boris Karloff) comforts the dying princess.

The waters showed pictures of events that happened 3,700 years ago.

A priest named Im-ho-tep loved Pharaoh's daughter, Ankh-es-en-amon, who was a priestess of the Goddess Isis. But the princess fell sick. In spite of all that Im-ho-tep could do, she died.

"We will meet again," Ankh-es-en-amon whispered. "In the Land of the Dead."

Im-ho-tep gazed on her dead body. Grief filled him. He resolved to do an unholy thing in order to bring his beloved back to life.

Im-ho-tep stole the sacred Scroll of Thoth. After Ankh-es-en-amon was mummified and placed in her tomb, Im-ho-tep broke in. He had his slaves lift the mummy of the princess out of its stone coffin.

Kneeling beside her, he began to recite the words on the scroll that would bring her back to life.

But he was discovered by Pharaoh's soldiers and taken prisoner. The ruler of Egypt said: "You have committed a terrible crime against our religion. Your punishment will be equally terrible. You will be buried alive. Since your body will not be prepared as a true mummy, you will never find eternal life!"

Im-ho-tep steals the scroll.

Slaves take Im-ho-tep and the scroll to the secret tomb.

Pharaoh's commands were obeyed. The casket with the living Im-ho-tep was taken to a secret tomb and put inside. Then the slaves who closed the tomb were killed, so that no one would know where Im-ho-tep was.

The Scroll of Thoth, which Im-ho-tep had sought to misuse, was buried with him. The Egyptians believed that Im-ho-tep's spirit would stay with his buried body, miserable forever, instead of enjoying happiness in the Land of the Dead . . .

Helen stared into the waters of the pool. In a strange voice, she said, "So once I was a princess, a servant of the Goddess Isis." She looked up. A statue of the goddess stood on one side of the room. On an altar nearby was the mummy of Ankh-es-en-amon.

Im-ho-tep said, "I cannot revive this mummy, which I stole from the museum. It would be only a heartless shell, since the spirit of my princess now dwells in you."

Stepping to the altar, the Egyptian set fire to the princess's mummy. Then he called his servants and had them take Helen away to dress her in the garments of Ankh-es-en-amon.

Im-ho-tep is about to set the princess's mummy on fire.

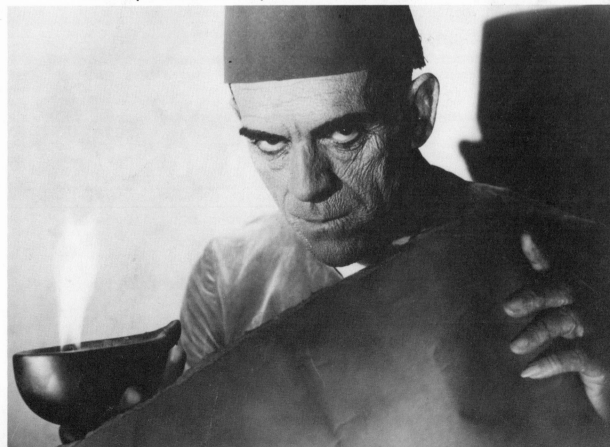

Im-ho-tep's servant (Noble Johnson) brings Helen to the altar of sacrifice.

"But, why?" cried Helen. "What are you going to do?"

"Give you eternal life," said Im-ho-tep. "But first, the body that you inhabit now must be sacrificed to the God of the Dead."

The Nubian servant brought Helen back in a short time. Now she was wearing the robes of an ancient Egyptian princess. The servant put Helen down before Im-ho-tep. Then he went away to prepare the chemicals that would turn her dead body into a mummy.

"Come, my beloved," said Im-ho-tep. He raised a glittering knife above Helen's heart.

Suddenly there was a crash. Frank and Dr. Muller burst into the room. They had been searching for Helen, and now they rushed to her rescue.

But Im-ho-tep raised his ring of power. The two men halted in their tracks, helpless. Im-ho-tep raised the knife again.

The spirit of the long-dead princess seemed to enter the body of Helen. She leaped up and ran to the statue of the Goddess Isis.

"Yes!" she cried. "I am Ankh-es-en-amon. But I am somebody else, too. I want to live, even in this strange new world. O Isis, save me!"

Im-ho-tep stood over her with the knife. The princess said, "Isis, save me from that mummy! It's dead!"

The stone hand of the statue moved. It held a cross-shaped amulet, and from it streamed a shining ray.

The ray struck Im-ho-tep. Instantly, the body of the terrible mummy crumbled away to dust. At the same time, the Scroll of Thoth caught fire and burned.

"Helen!" cried Frank, taking her into his arms. "Helen — come back!"

For an instant, the spirit of Ankh-es-en-amon looked out of the girl's eyes. And then Helen herself clung to Frank, safe at last from the mummy's power.

THE MUMMY'S HAND

The original movie about the mummy inspired many others. They were not as well done as the Karloff film, but they can be exciting to watch, even today.

In 1940, moviegoers met, for the first time, an evil mummy named Kharis. Like Im-ho-tep, he had been buried alive for daring to meddle with the mummy of a princess. In this film the High Priests of Karnak, in Egypt, guarded the hidden tomb of Princess Ananka. In modern times, it seemed that scientists would find the tomb and shame Ananka by putting her mummy in a museum.

The priest Andoheb is given a secret mission: to destroy the scientists. His weapon will be an avenging mummy!

For Kharis never really died. Over thousands of years, the Priests of Karnak have kept him sleeping in his coffin. The juice of forbidden tana leaves revives the mummy. But he must never be given more than the juice of nine leaves . . . or the mummy will become an uncontrollable monster.

Andoheb spies on the scientific expedition. The mummy is sent to kill first one person, and then another. The wicked Andoheb plans to do away with everyone except Marta, daughter of the expedition's backer. Marta will be made immortal by means of tana juice, and share the priesthood of Andoheb.

A young scientist named Steve Banning finds Marta gone. She has been stolen away by the mummy. Steve and his sidekick, a man named Babe, rush into the temple and find Marta menaced by Andoheb.

Kharis the Mummy (Tom Tyler) carries off Marta (Peggy Moran) in a scene from *The Mummy's Hand.*

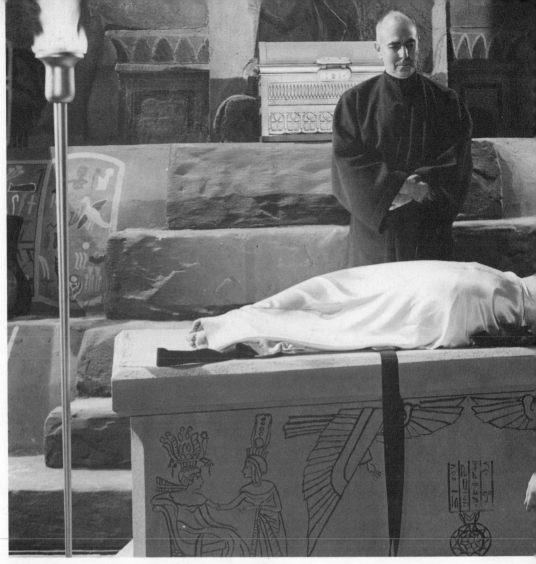

The Mummy watches Marta inside the temple.

Shots ring out. The wicked Andoheb falls. But his slave, the mummy Kharis, comes lurching after Steve. He flings the young man to the floor. What Kharis really seeks is the bowl filled with tana juice. If the mummy drinks this, he will obtain superhuman powers.

"Don't let him get the tana juice!" Steve cries.

Babe fires and hits the bowl. The precious juice falls to the floor and the mummy tries to scoop it up.

What can Steve do? Babe's bullets do not harm the monster. Steve throws a torch . . .

Instantly the mummy bursts into flame. It seems to be finished. Steve, Babe and Marta flee from the temple as the film ends.

But Kharis was to good a villain to perish. He returned in a new movie two years later. It was called *The Mummy's Tomb.*

Mehemet (Turhan Bey) tells the Mummy (Lon Chaney, Jr.) to get out of his tomb in a scene from The Mummy's Tomb.

THE MUMMY'S TOMB

Twenty years have gone by. Steve Banning is now an old man. His son John and John's fiancee, Isobel, listen as Steve tells them the story of Kharis.

The young people scoff when the story is ended. Walking mummies! What silly superstition.

Meanwhile, in Egypt, the High Priest Andoheb speaks to his young successor, Mehemet. (Andoheb was not killed by Babe's bullets, only wounded.) The dying old villain makes Mehemet promise to seek revenge on the Banning family. Mehemet secretly takes the mummy of Kharis to the United States.

Soon the mummy is running wild in Massachusetts, first killing people, and then running off with the beautiful Isobel, whom Mehemet has fallen in love with.

In an action-filled climax, John Banning shoots Mehemet and rescues Isobel. Then he pursues the mummy, who again snatches up the girl. John seizes a burning torch from one of the townspeople who came to hunt down the mummy. He corners the monster inside the Banning house, and sets the place on fire. The young man and woman escape from the inferno . . . the burning building collapses on Kharis and seems to put an end to him.

But wait! Movie fans wanted more mummy movies. And in 1944, they got a real thriller. *The Mummy's Ghost* may be the best of the Kharis films.

John Banning (John Hubbard) waves a torch at the Mummy.

Anadoheb (George Zucco) orders Youssef Bey (John Carradine) to go to America in The Mummy's Ghost *(1944).*

THE MUMMY'S GHOST

It opens in Egypt. Once again we see Andoheb, and again he seems to be dying. This time the revenge order is passed to a sinister fellow named Youssef Bey, who is ordered to go to America and summon the mummy's ghost. He is also to reclaim the mummy of Princess Ananka, which has been sent to a museum in New England.

At a college near the museum, a professor has been experimenting unwisely with tana leaves. The smell of the magical brew is enough to arouse Kharis from wherever he has been buried. He kills the professor.

Then Kharis hears a mysterious call. Youssef Bey has arrived, and the mummy must act as his slave. Hurrying to where Youssef awaits, Kharis passes a car. Inside are two college students, Tom and Amina. She is a student from Egypt. Soon we will learn that the spirt of the Princess Ananka resides in Amina's lovely body.

Youssef gives a potion of life-giving tana juice to the Mummy (Lon Chaney, Jr.).

The mummy comes to Youssef Bey in the museum. And there Kharis sees the mummy of his beloved Ananka! He leans over to embrace her, but she crumbles to dust.

At the same moment, miles away, the girl Amina wakes up screaming.

Now Amina undergoes a mysterious change. Her hair turns to silver. She refuses to have anything to do with Tom. The evil Youssef realizes that Ananka's spirit has gone fully into Amina. He plans to take Amina for himself.

The Mummy and Youssef watch Amina's (Ramsay Ames) hair change color.

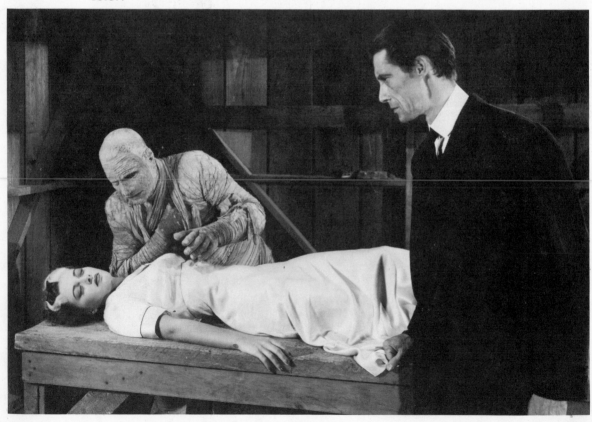

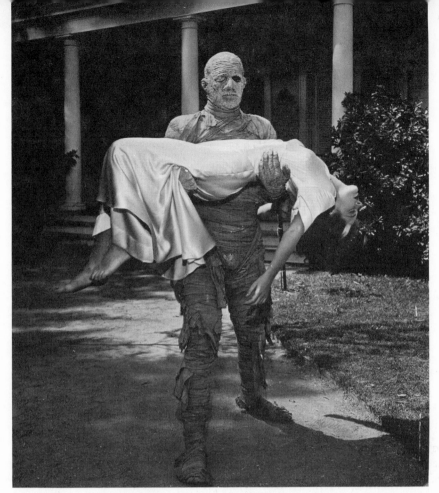

The Mummy carries Amina away from the house.

Kharis turns on his former master and kills him. Taking Amina into his bandaged arms, Kharis flees as Tom and other townspeople come to rescue the girl.

Kharis takes Amina into a dangerous swamp. With every passing moment, the girl in the mummy's arms grows older and older. The Princess Ananka, after all, was more than three thousand years old.

At last, Kharis steps into a murky pool. He and his beloved begin to sink. In a last heart-rending scene, we see the two doomed, wrinkled forms vanish into the depths as Tom looks on, horrified.

OTHER MUMMIES

A fourth Kharis movie was made in 1945. *The Mummy's Curse* was a stale film, and so the famous monster was "put on the shelf" for awhile. He reappeared in a comedy, *Abbott and Costello Meet the Mummy*, in 1955.

An entirely new group of mummy films, this time made in color, began in 1959. The British horror-film studio, Hammer Films, which re-made many classics, brought out a stylish version of *The Mummy* in 1959. It starred Christopher Lee as Kharis and Peter Cushing as John Banning. Its plot was similar to that of *The Mummy's Hand*.

The modern film was much more gruesome than the black-and-white original. It was followed by several sequels that were full of gore and violence.

Most horror film fans believe that the modern mummy films are not as well-done as the great classic that starred Boris Karloff. With his deep eyes and hypnotic voice, Karloff made you believe that he was more than three thousand years old. You shudder as you look at that eery, wrinkled face.

Dr. Muller says: "The gods of Egypt still live in these hills, in their ruined temples. The ancient spells have weakened, but some of them are still strong."

Looking at Karloff, as Im-ho-tep the Mummy, you can believe it!

Boris Karloff as Im-ho-tep the Mummy talks to Helen in the original mummy movie, *The Mummy.*

DATE DUE

	JUL 2 5 1988	
	SEP 9 1989	
	MAR 1 4 1990	
	MAR 1 3 1990	
	MAR 1 8 1991	
	JUL 1 7 1991	
	AUG 2 4 1991	
	SEP 0 7 1992	
	SEP 1 6 1992	
	SEP 0 9 1994	
	MAY 0 9 1996	
	NOV 0 3 1996	
	JUL 2 7 1998	
	JAN 2 7 '00	
	JAN 29 '03	
	NOV 1 8 '03	
	MAR 2 0 04	
AUG. 1 3 1987		
OCT 2 1 1987		
DEC 2 1 1987		
MAR 2 3 1995		
JUN - 3 1985		
AUG. 2 9 1985		
SEP. 1 0 1985		
OCT 2 - 1985		
OCT 2 1 1985		
JUL 1 5 1986		
JUN 2 9 1986		
JUL 29 1986		
MAR 2 1 1987		
MAY 1 8 1987		
JUN 25 1987		
JUL 2 2 1987		
OCT 1 9 1987		

DEMCO NO. 38-298